"The monster within me"
Surviving sickle cell disease

Written by: Juanita McClain

Illustrated by: Dwight Nacaytuna

To order additional copies of this book, contact:
Xlibris
1-888-795-4274
www.Xlibris.com
Orders@Xlibris.com

Dedication:

This book is a dedicated to my son Antonio Soto who passed away during my struggle of battling sickle cell disease. Also to my sons Aaden and Ronald for being my motivation and inspiration. And most importantly God for keeping my alive and giving me the strength to go on and inspire others.

Hello, my name is Juanita

I was born here at Children's hospital

I live with my mom, dad, my big sister
Shontea and baby sister Jasmine.

My mom and dad were born with sickle cell trait

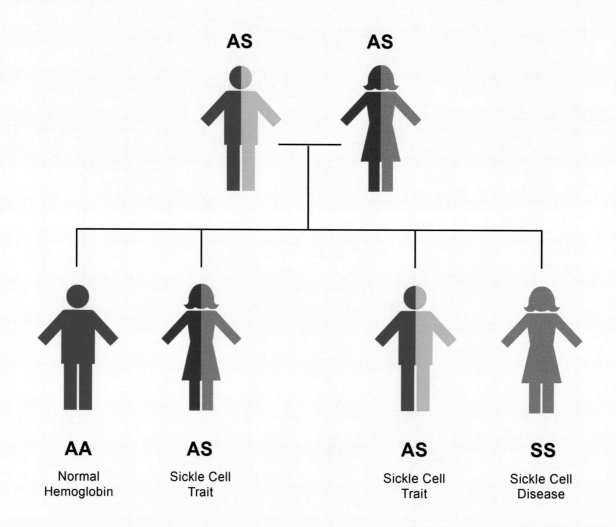

AA
Normal
Hemoglobin

AS
Sickle Cell
Trait

AS
Sickle Cell
Trait

SS
Sickle Cell
Disease

Which caused me to be born with this monster that lives inside of me called sickle cell disease.

When my red blood cells are not getting enough oxygen they become deformed into a "sickle" shape.

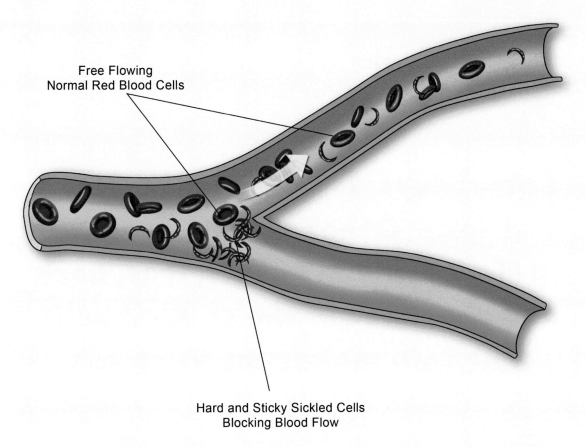

Free Flowing
Normal Red Blood Cells

Hard and Sticky Sickled Cells
Blocking Blood Flow

The sickle shape cells are hard and sticky.

The hard and sticky cells makes it hard for them to travel to the rest of my body which causes me to have a sickle cell crises which is no fun.

Some days I feel really tired, and lazy. Other days I feel pain in places like my arms, legs, back and chest from the sickled cells. The pain makes me very sad.

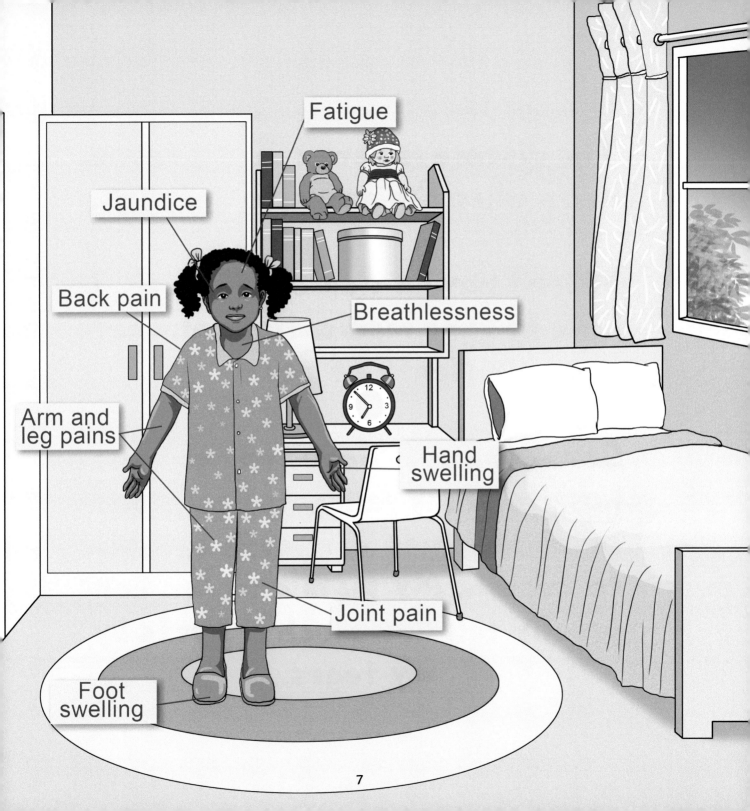

Fatigue

Jaundice

Back pain

Breathlessness

Arm and
leg pains

Hand
swelling

Joint pain

Foot
swelling

The disease is very scary. I never know when I'm going to get sick.

When I have a sickle cell crisis, I have to take medications and get plenty of rest.

Sometimes I have to go the hospital if my pain gets really bad or it becomes difficult for me to breath. My mom and dad can usually tell how much it hurts by my tears.

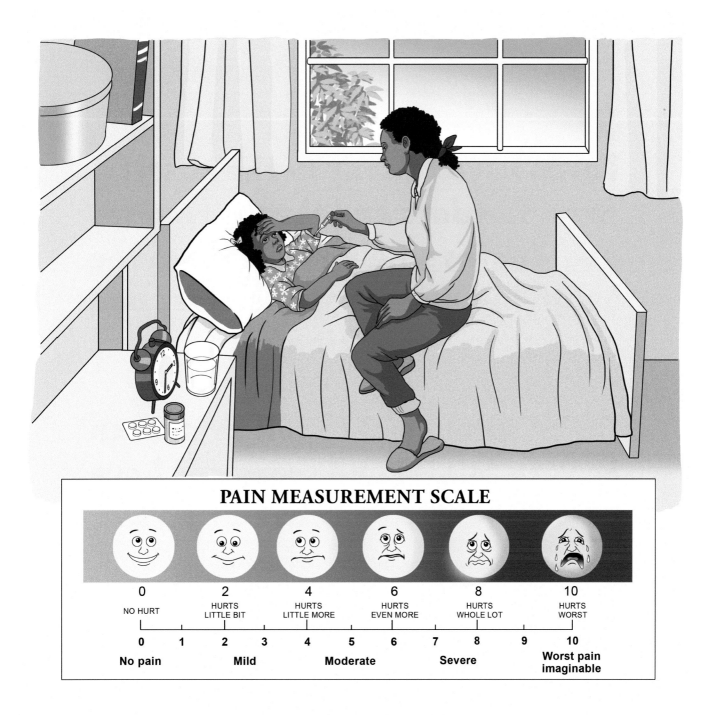

PAIN MEASUREMENT SCALE

0	2	4	6	8	10
NO HURT	HURTS LITTLE BIT	HURTS LITTLE MORE	HURTS EVEN MORE	HURTS WHOLE LOT	HURTS WORST

0   1   2   3   4   5   6   7   8   9   10

No pain   **Mild**   **Moderate**   **Severe**   **Worst pain imaginable**

I even have to stay in the hospital for a few days and the nice nurses and doctors help me feel better by giving me oxygen, fluids, and medicine.

Going into a sickle cell crisis can be very painful and scary so I have to take very good care of myself to prevent them.

When it's hot I drink plenty of water to help me stay hydrated.

When it's cold I dress really warm so the cold doesn't make me go into a sickle cell crises.

I take vitamins every morning when I wake up. I also go to the clinic often for a check up to make sure my health is on the right track.

And all of those things helps me stay healthy.

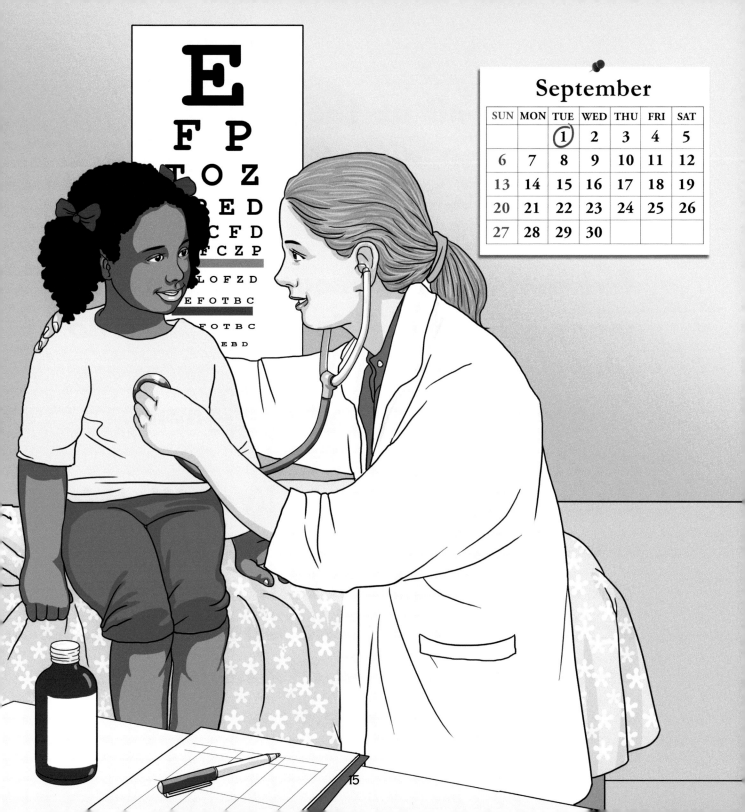

I can't do all of the fun things my friends can without going into a sickle cell crisis.

But that is okay because there are so many other fun things that I can do like playing with my toys, coloring, reading, and even play games.

Even though I have to live with this monster within me, I am still like everyone else. I can still play, do fun activities, travel the world, and go as far as I want in life as long as I put my mind to it.

"However difficult life may seem, there is always something you can do and succeed at."

Stephen Hawking

Important Terms and Definitions:

Sickle cell disease- A blood disorder caused by an inherited abnormal hemoglobin. The red blood cells become distorted into a "sickled" shape at low oxygen levels.

Hemoglobin- The oxygen- carrying protein within the red blood cells.
Inherited- genetically from one's parents or ancestors.

Penicillin- group of antibiotics used to treat a large range of bacterial infections.

Folic acid- Helps the body produce and maintain new cells.

Hydroxyurea- used in adult patients with sickle cell anemia to prevent painful episodes and reduce the need for blood transfusions.

Sickle cell trait- a condition in which a child inherits the sickle cell gene mutation from one parent.

References:
Center for disease control and prevention. "Sickle cell". 17 Nov. 2016; accessed: Jan. 2017 http://www.CDC.gov

Printed in the United States
By Bookmasters